MARGRET & H.A.REY'S
Curious George
Saves His Pennies

Written by Monica Perez

Illustrated by Mary O'Keefe Young

HOUGHTON MIFFLIN HARCOURT
Boston   New York

George was a good little monkey and always very curious, especially when he was in Tammy's Toy Store.

There were so many things to wonder about . . .
pogo sticks and skateboards,

snow globes
and kaleidoscopes,

and even finger traps.

But George's favorite thing to do in the
toy store was play at the train table.
Today there was a new train.
Its wood was painted bright
red, and it had a real
working whistle.

George held it up to show his friend, the man with the yellow hat. "Not today," his friend said.

"We're looking for a birthday present for Noah, remember? He's turning five. What do you think of this?"

George helped his friend pick out
a yellow and green hula hoop.
While Tammy the shopkeeper
wrapped the present for the
birthday party, George
wandered back to
the train table.

"I have a suggestion, George," said the man as he carried the gift over.

"Why don't you buy that new train yourself? The tag says $5.00. I'm sure you can save the money for it."

George liked this suggestion so much that he was only a little sorry to put the train back down.

George had a good time at the birthday party. Noah let everyone have a turn at the hula hoop. It was harder than it looked!

As soon as George got home that afternoon, he took his piggy bank down from his dresser. He opened the small plug at the bottom and shook. Out tumbled a nickel. George ran to show the coin to his friend.

"You have five cents," the man said. "I'll give you your allowance early this week. Don't spend it on candy. You have to save it up." The man gave George two quarters.

"Here is fifty cents," he said. "Now you have fifty-five cents. You have only $4.45 left to save."

George wasn't quite sure how much money that was, but it sounded like a lot.

George dreamed about his red train that night. He was riding it through a forest of trees. He tugged on the whistle again and again so that no one could miss such a shiny red engine!

In the morning, George decided he would have to find a way to earn money faster. What if someone else were to buy the red train at the toy store before he could?

He had an idea.

George found five pennies and a dime in the sofa cushions.

He found a nickel under his bed.

His piggy bank jingled nicely that evening.
He had seventy-five cents saved. One more
quarter and he would have a dollar!

The next morning George had another idea. He would get a job.

Lucky for George, his neighbor Mr. Reddy needed help raking leaves. George worked all morning long, gathering armfuls of red, brown, and gold leaves to add to a growing pile in the center of the yard. Mr. Reddy brought out lemonade for the two to share. While his neighbor rested on the sun porch swing, George climbed a tree.

The pile of leaves looked tempting from above.
George wondered what would happen if . . .

Before he finished wondering, he had swung out of the branches and right into the center of the pile. The leaves crunched and crumbled and swooshed and swirled. What an adventure!

What hard work it was raking the leaves back up!

But at the end of the day, Mr. Reddy paid him two dollars. George had $2.75 saved. That was almost three dollars.

George spent many days doing odd jobs.

He washed windows.

He distributed flyers.

He delivered flowers.

He did dishes.

At the end of a week, George
finally had $5.00.

"I'm proud of you, George,"
said the man with the
yellow hat.

"You saved all that money
by yourself. You've sure earned
that train."

The change clinked merrily in the piggy bank as George set off
for the toy store. The autumn day was bright and clear and not
very cold. George walked by the park.

The neighborhood children were playing with a windsock. Suddenly, it got stuck in a tree. They needed George's help!

George carefully set his piggy bank down on a nearby park bench where he could keep an eye on it. But little monkeys sometimes forget. And as George began to play with the children, he forgot to check that his bank was still there.

As the afternoon wore on, his friends went home to have dinner. George rushed to the park bench where he had left his piggy bank. The toy store might be closing soon. But his bank was gone!

Maybe George had the wrong bench?

There were many in
the park, after all.

But he was disappointed each time
he ran up to another empty bench.

George walked home sadly. He wondered how long it would take him to save five dollars again. As George passed the toy store, he happened to look through the window. He couldn't believe his eyes. A little girl was holding his piggy bank!

George rushed into the toy store just as the girl's mother was saying, "We found this across the street and waited for its owner, but it's getting late. We saw it has the name of your store on the bottom. Can you keep it in case someone comes to claim it?"

George jumped up and down on the counter. "Why, George!" Tammy said. "Is the piggy bank yours? You're lucky Hana and her mother found it."

Hugging his piggy bank tightly, George rushed over to the train section. He located the shiny red engine right away.

As he carried it to the counter, the little girl looked at his train shyly.

George realized he had not said thank you to her for keeping
his savings safe. He looked at his train. He looked at his piggy bank. He
looked at Hana. Good deeds deserve to be rewarded, he decided. George
set the train down. He upended his bank on
the counter and began to sort
dollars and coins.

George and Hana walked out of the toy store that day each carrying a train. George's small engine was not red, but it was shiny and blue and he had paid for it all by himself. Best of all, he had a new friend who loved to play with trains almost as much as he did.